Killer Style

HOW FASHION HAS INJURED, MAIMED, & MURDERED THROUGH HISTORY

BY **SERAH-MARIE MCMAHON**
& **ALISON MATTHEWS DAVID**

ILLUSTRATIONS BY **GILLIAN WILSON**

OWLKIDS BOOKS

Contents

Fashion Victims

Famous fashion designer Oscar de la Renta coined the term "fashion victims" to describe the kinds of consumers who blindly follow fads, love logos, and wear whatever style dictates. They are the victims of marketing departments and advertising agencies, convinced to spend endless dollars on whatever is declared the newest, the trendiest, the hottest must-have fashion item.

This book is certainly full of fashion victims matching de la Renta's description, but more importantly, it is also filled with literal victims. It is about people who have suffered physical pain, injury, and worse, attempting to look more attractive, or to make others look more attractive. This book is about when fashion kills.

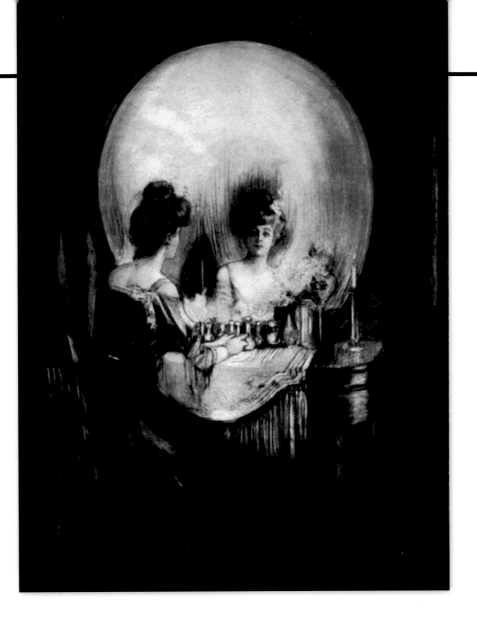

And it turns out, there are lots of ways for fashion to be fatal. Fabrics can burst into flame or become infested with disease-carrying bugs. Clothing can constrict, trip, tangle, and strangle. A scarf can behead; a hatter can be driven mad. Something as simple as a specific shade of green can sap away life.

At the most basic level, we rely on clothing to protect us in our daily lives. It comforts us and shields us from the elements. And we like to think of grooming activities, such as dyeing our hair and putting on makeup, as pampering ourselves or showing our best face to the world. But you might be surprised to find out that from the tops of our heads to the tips of our toes, the things we put on to look good can turn out to be very, very bad.

Part One

Horrified Heads

Murderous Mercury Hats

What is the best way to construct a gravity-defying hat like Blackbeard's jaunty tricorn, Abraham Lincoln's towering stovepipe, or Cap'n Crunch's tribute to Napoleon? Mold it out of felt, a fabric traditionally made by wetting animal fur and matting its fibers together.

For centuries, it was socially unacceptable for European men to leave the house hatless, and as a result, felt was in constant demand. Beaver fur was a popular choice, but eventually the supply dwindled. Rabbit fur was cheap and plentiful, but turning it into felt was difficult and time-consuming.

In the 1730s, hatmakers discovered that if you added just a little mercury to even the cheapest furs, they would easily transform into felt. The problem of pricey hats was finally resolved.

Too bad mercury is totally toxic.

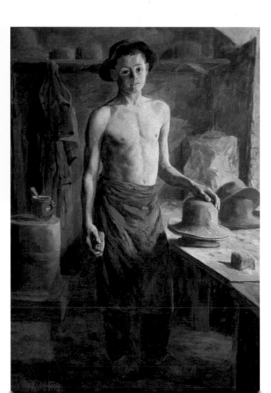

Boys started as apprentices in hot and dirty hatting workshops, sanding hats and inhaling toxic mercury dust all day long.

Fantastic Hats and How to Make Them

Mercury is a metal that stays in liquid form at room temperature and can be absorbed through the skin. Hats made with mercury were coated in shellac and lined with silk and leather, so hat-wearers were safe. However, it was impossible for hatmakers to avoid the toxic metal. By 1825, Parisian workers were making almost two million hats annually. Each hatter would personally come into contact with twenty-two pounds (ten kilograms) of mercury every year—the same weight as two thousand melted quarters.

Years of mercury exposure left hatters with some strange symptoms. Their gums shrank dramatically, and two out

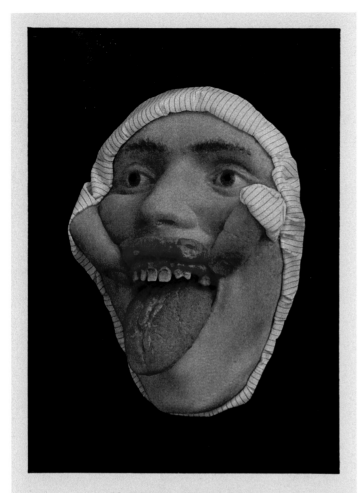

No. 91. Stomatitis mercurialis.

This wax model of a real victim's face shows mercury-damaged lips, teeth, and tongue—a dentist's nightmare.

THE MYTH OF THE MAD HATTER

The famous fictional Mad Hatter character is from Lewis Carroll's 1865 novel, *Alice's Adventures in Wonderland*. He is described as sporting an oversized top hat, reciting nonsense poetry, and hosting a never-ending tea party without any tea.

Carroll grew up near Stockport, UK, a hotbed of hatmaking, and he was probably exposed to the common sight of disturbed and confused hatters. So some speculate that the Mad Hatter was suffering from mercury poisoning. But others disagree. Those suffering from mercury madness were usually intensely shy and wanted to be invisible—the opposite of Alice's hyper host.

of every three lost all their teeth. Occasionally their tongues swelled so much they couldn't close their mouths. They smelled like metal all the time. Their eyelids, and eventually their limbs, would tremble and convulse. Many hatters would develop paranoid personalities, becoming extremely irritable and withdrawn.

Despite all the evidence, nothing was ever really done to protect hatters. It was only when hats became unfashionable in the 1960s that the production of felt tapered off. Mercury was never officially banned in England, and it was regulated in the US only in the 1990s. Far too late to help the hatters.

Catastrophic Comb Bombs

Before "tortoiseshell" was a way to describe the blond-and-brown pattern on a pair of plastic glasses, it was the name of a material made from the underbelly of a rare sea turtle. Highly prized for its polished, translucent quality, tortoiseshell was used to make jewelry, hair combs, and other accessories. It was also exceedingly expensive.

In 1856, a British inventor named Alexander Parkes created an early form of synthetic plastic—what we now call celluloid. At first, the revolutionary material was used for toys, billiard balls, and photo film. After a while, people figured out it could also imitate all the qualities of tortoiseshell, at a fraction of the price.

Only one problem: celluloid had a tendency to explode.

The Hazards of Celluloid in the Factory

Manufacturing celluloid products was a tricky, treacherous practice. The temperature that renders celluloid soft and moldable is nearly the same as the temperature that makes it burst into flames. Even the smallest spark could ignite an inferno, so employees at celluloid factories were fired just for having matches in their pockets. Despite rigorous

Victorian girls used pretty, inexpensive celluloid combs not to untangle their hair but as fashion accessories to decorate their long locks.

precautions, the accident rate was high. The New Jersey Celluloid Manufacturing Company was alarmingly unlucky; over the course of thirty-six years, it suffered thirty-nine fires and nine fatalities.

...And in the Store

The blame for England's biggest department store fire in history belongs to celluloid and bad decorating choices.

During the 1909 holiday season, a festive window was crammed with celluloid hair accessories and fake snow made from cotton wool. The combination would prove explosive. When a clerk reached for a comb, he accidentally knocked over a lamp and instantly ignited the entire display. In less than ten minutes, all five floors of the store went up in flames and nine employees perished in the blaze, which went on to destroy another forty shops and homes.

...And at Home

Demand for the fantastic plastic nonetheless increased, and manufacturers started releasing products made of cheaper, even less stable celluloid. These items didn't need open flame to explode; enough heat alone could ignite catastrophe.

Newspapers alerted the public to exploding celluloid by reporting close calls, like the case of "Mademoiselle T." The young French girl was next to a hot coal heater when her hair comb ignited, and she nearly lost her life. Celluloid fires claimed victims into the 1920s and 1930s, when the material was finally replaced by less flammable plastic alternatives.

Dangers of the dressing-room

It is at all times a dangerous practice to use an unprotected light on the dressing-table, but more so if your brush and comb have any celluloid about them. In an instant, before you are aware of it, they may catch alight

Newspapers warned about the dangers of celluloid so that people were aware of the risks. At the same time, Victorian girls' magazines suggested "fun" science experiments, such as putting your hair comb in a fireplace and watching it explode. (Don't try this at home!)

Dangerous Hair Dye

Humans have been changing the color of their hair for more than ten thousand years. Archaeologists discovered that early humans used rust to redden their hair in the Stone Age. Thousands of years later, ancient Romans made black hair dye by soaking leeches in red wine for forty days. And to cover up grays? They prepared a mixture of boiled walnut shells and charred earthworms.

Modern hair dye might be a little less gross, but it can also be a lot more lethal. A whopping 99 percent of hair dye includes an ingredient with a very long name: para-phenylenediamine, called PPD for short. It's currently the only known substance that will stick to gray hair.

It also causes powerful, sometimes deadly, allergic reactions in about 1 percent of the population.

Dye Hard

About twice as many people are allergic to PPD as peanuts. But unlike a peanut allergy, a reaction to PPD can develop at any time—even if you've been dying your hair for years without incident. Common reactions include a cracked, blistered scalp and a swollen face. Uncommon reactions include blindness and, occasionally, death.

In the 1930s, a high dose of PPD was added to a product called Lash Lure, used to dye eyebrows and lashes. Allergic reactions to Lash Lure killed at least eighteen people and permanently blinded others.

PPD is now banned in makeup. However, it is still allowed as an ingredient in hair dye sold around the world. And it continues to cause damage. In 2011, a seventeen-year-old Scottish girl named Tabatha McCourt dyed her hair, as she had done many times before. Only this time, she had a severe allergic reaction and stopped

breathing less than twenty minutes after applying the product. This reaction is extremely rare, but it's why manufacturers recommend a patch test every single time you dye your hair.

In 1933, American Hazel Fay Brown had her lashes and brows dyed with Lash Lure, suffered a severe allergic reaction, and was blinded forever.

DYING TO BE BLOND

In the 1930s, Hollywood starlet Jean Harlow was renowned for her "platinum blond" hair. The hairstyle required a weekly application of ammonia and bleach. Together, these two ingredients create hydrochloric acid, a substance strong enough to remove rust from steel. When its fumes are inhaled, it causes kidney damage. Harlow's kidneys were already weakened by a teenage bout with scarlet fever, but it's possible that her hazardous hairdo caused them to fail completely.

Lethal Lead Makeup

Lead is one of the densest metals in existence, yet it is soft and melts easily. It clings fantastically to skin, feels smooth and thick, and shows colors brightly. These qualities make lead an ideal substance for cosmetics, and for thousands of years, lead has been liberally applied to eyes, mouths, and skin.

The downside? Lead can build up in your bones and damage almost every organ system in your body.

Black Lead

HOW IT'S MADE: Lead is extracted from a dark silvery-gray rock called galena.

EXAMPLE OF COSMETIC USE: Kohl

In ancient Egypt, galena was ground up and mixed with water to form a dark, thick paste called kohl. Men and women used it to line their eyes, and the paste became popular throughout the world, especially in West Africa, South Asia, and the Middle East.

A 1991 American study tested twenty-two samples of store-bought kohl, and seven of them contained more than 50 percent lead. To confuse things, many modern makeup brands use the word "kohl" to describe the color of a product, even when it's lead-free. To avoid lead liner, make sure to only buy makeup with the ingredients clearly listed.

White Lead

HOW IT'S MADE: Lead is soaked in vinegar then dried out, leaving a remarkably opaque white powder.

EXAMPLE OF COSMETIC USE: Ceruse

Ancient Romans were pretty creative with their skincare. They dabbed a mixture of chicken fat and onions onto pimples. They tried using the ashes of fish bones to remove freckles. A very popular face mask was made with … crocodile poop.

Ceruse must have seemed downright healthy compared to these concoctions, and people regularly painted it all over their faces to give themselves a smooth, blemish-free look. Sadly, it caused the skin to age rapidly and erupt with sores, requiring more ceruse to cover up these new imperfections.

Even once these side effects were well known, ceruse remained popular for centuries. When Queen Elizabeth I was twenty-nine years old, she came down with a nasty case of smallpox. She survived the illness but was noticeably scarred. For the rest of her life, she painted a thick layer of ceruse on her face, neck, and hands—a practice many believe hastened her demise in 1603.

Red Lead

HOW IT'S MADE: White lead is exposed to extremely high temperatures.

EXAMPLE OF COSMETIC USE: Sindoor

Some Hindu women apply this red pigment along the part of their hair and to place a red bindi on their forehead. Traditionally, sindoor was made from the nontoxic bark of the sindoor tree. But modern incarnations are often colored with red lead. In 2008, the brand Swad issued a massive recall of sindoor due to lead levels as high as 87 percent. In 2017, Rutgers University tested 118 samples of sindoor. Shockingly, 83 percent included lead, with one-third containing levels above the US Food and Drug Administration safety limit.

Strangling Scarves

In the 1970s, American craniofacial surgeon Dr. Mutaz Habal was concerned about a fashion trend. Inspired by time-traveling television character Doctor Who, folks had taken to bundling up with long, winding scarves to keep warm while playing winter sports. And it was killing them.

Dozens of these scarves got tangled in moving snowmobiles and ski chairlifts, strangling their owners. Dr. Habal invented the medical-sounding term "Long Scarf Syndrome," helping the wholly preventable problem to be taken seriously.

But the problem persists. A 2016 study by Dr. Zafarullah Beigh in India used the same term to point out the high rate of chunnis (six-foot-long scarves popular with South Asian women) getting caught in motorbikes and farming equipment.

Hanging by a Thread

Celebrated American dancer Isadora Duncan was perhaps the most famous person to succumb to neckwear. One evening in 1927, she climbed into the back seat of a convertible, wrapped her signature long shawl twice around her neck, and flung it over her shoulder. As she waved goodbye, she shouted what would be her final words: "Farewell, my friends. I go to glory!" As the driver sped off, he didn't notice that the long fringes of Duncan's shawl had wrapped around the back wheel of the car. She nearly lost her head and definitely lost her life.

Isadora Duncan became a legend after death—plays, operas, movies, and rock songs were written about her. She even gets a tribute in the Series of Unfortunate Events book series: the first two Quagmire triplets are named Isadora and Duncan.

TRAGIC TALES OF ENTANGLEMENT

Anything dangling from the neck has the devastating potential to cause peril.
Here are some examples of fun turning fatal.

SLIDE

Michigan, US, 1994: Five-year-old Nancy Sibley was playing on a spiral slide when the drawstring of her winter coat snagged and strangled her. Since then, Sibley's mother has successfully convinced thirty-three leading makers of kids' clothing to ban drawstrings from their products.

DOG

New York, US, 2006: Six-year-old Kaitlyn Hassard was playing in her backyard with her family's golden retriever. The dog grabbed her three-foot-long scarf in its mouth and dragged her a short distance, tightening the scarf around her neck and accidentally suffocating her.

GO-KART

Northeastern Turkey, 2017: Twenty-one-year-old Tuğba Cevahir was go-kart racing when her hijab came loose, tangling in the back wheel and causing her to crash. Fortunately, track staff rushed immediately to her aid, and she survived.

Part Two

Miserable Middles

Constricting Corsets

Some trends are easier to follow than others. If cerulean blue comes into style, it's relatively easy to purchase a cerulean blue sweater. But what happens when a body shape becomes fashionable? Hip-to-waist ratio isn't simply for sale.

Humans have long used clothing to change their silhouettes, exaggerating and accentuating different features. Depending on the era, trends have favored flattened or overflowing chests, cinched or straight waists, and flared or narrow hips.

Starting in the late sixteenth century, people used to manipulate their middles by wearing a corset. The garment's stiff fabric was made even more rigid with whalebone and later metal, and it laced up like a running shoe. Though always fitted, the corset could also be "tight-laced" to dramatically compress the body and deliver a startlingly smaller waist.

Corsets weren't just wildly popular—they were also controversial. From the moment they came into style, experts have blamed them for all kinds of ailments—physical, mental, and social.

Some have even accused the corset of murder.

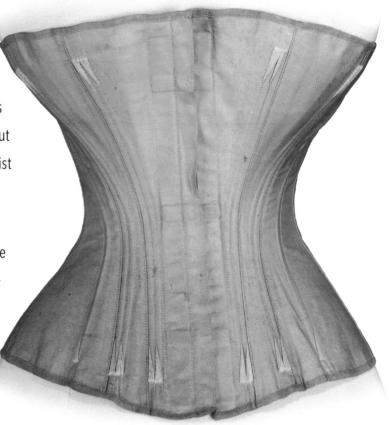

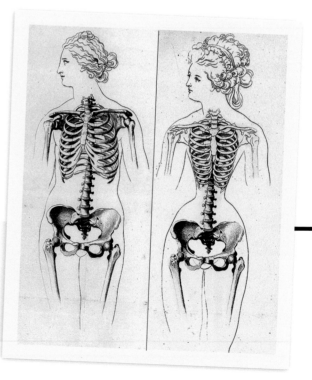

Starting in the eighteenth century, male doctors and the popular press shared overdramatic images of corsets harming and even killing women who supposedly laced them too tightly.

Killer Corset Controversy

Does this body wrap deserve its bad rap? Let's sort out fact from fiction.

CRUSHED LUNGS ... TRUE!

Very tight corsets can cause shortness of breath because the lower parts of the lungs are unable to fully expand and contract. Fainting is not uncommon.

DEFORMED RIB CAGE ... TRUE! AND FALSE!

Constant corset-wear can permanently deform the still-growing bones of a young person. However, the ribs of fully grown adults will return to place once the garment is removed.

REMOVED RIBS ... FALSE!

Tales are told of Victorian women surgically removing ribs to achieve a tiny waist. Fashion historian Valerie Steele dedicated years looking for a credible record of the procedure, to no avail. Before the invention of anesthetic and antibiotics, chest surgery was impossibly treacherous. The tales are tall.

DEATH ... FALSE!

A few centuries-old medical records claim corsets as a cause of death. However, we now know that these mortalities were more likely due to diseases that were little understood at the time.

TIGHT-LACING UP WITH THE KARDASHIANS

Corsets became news again in 2016, when the reality-TV family the Kardashians were paid to promote a line of "waist trainers." Their social media posts claimed the products would radically reduce your waist size. Even though waist trainers have been medically proven to be a waste of money, the hashtag #waisttraining has appeared upward of a million times on Instagram as of 2018.

Alarming Lice

One in ten kids ends up itchy with head lice at one time or another. These bugs are annoying, but they won't kill you. The same can't be said for head lice's bigger, badder cousins: body lice.

Body lice live and lay eggs in the seams of clothing, where it's nice and cozy, and move to the body for mealtimes. While they feed off their host's blood, they have a nasty habit of leaving behind a dangerous disease: typhus.

A Russian poster from 1919 depicts a typhus louse and Death as "friends and comrades."

Grim Lice Epidemics

Typhus is a bacterial infection that causes fever, muscle aches, and aggressive rashes, eventually leading to the fatal swelling of the heart and brain. It spreads fastest when people are crowded together, which is most common during times of famine and war. During these times, the number of deaths due to typhus has vastly outnumbered deaths by starvation and combat.

Of all the ways clothing can be deadly, providing a home for body lice is by far the deadliest.

THE GRANADA WAR, 1482–1492

Though typhus is likely an ancient affliction, the earliest recorded outbreak was during the final battle of this ten-year war. The king of Aragon (now a part of Spain) lost a total of twenty thousand soldiers: three thousand killed by the enemy and seventeen thousand by typhus.

A French soldier picks body lice out of his shirt by hand during the First World War. American soldiers used to call these bugs cooties, and they invented funny songs and dances, like "The Cootie Tickle" and "The March of the Cooties."

IRISH MIGRATION, 1847

In 1847, at the height of the Potato Famine, close to 110,000 Irish men, women, and children fled starvation in their homeland by packing themselves onto ships and sailing to Canada. The overcrowded "coffin ships" were ideal breeding grounds for lice. In a single year, nearly twenty thousand newly arrived Irish would die from typhus.

ETHIOPIAN FAMINE, 1983–1985

After record-low rainfalls caused total crop failure in northern Ethiopia, the government tried to stem the spreading starvation by moving everybody south. The mass migration led to overcrowding and made it difficult to wash clothes—the perfect conditions for body lice. In addition to brutal famine, Ethiopia suffered fourteen thousand cases of typhus—the most significant outbreak since the Second World War.

NO MORE MR. LICE GUY

In the early 1900s, French scientist Charles Nicolle noticed that the spread of typhus stopped once patients bathed and were given fresh clothes. In his lab, he was able to prove it definitively: hot water is all it takes to kill body lice and prevent an epidemic.

Unfortunately, hot water was in pretty short supply on the battlefield. The First World War started soon after Nicolle's discovery, leading to one of the most devastating typhus epidemics in history. As many as thirty million people in Eastern Europe succumbed to the disease.

Thankfully we now have a treatment for typhus. Still, the most powerful preventative remains the washing machine.

Flaming Flannelette

In the late Victorian era, it was widely believed that heat could not only prevent but actually cure illness. Flannel manufacturers, wanting to capitalize on the textile's ability to retain body heat, claimed it had healing properties that would miraculously cure ailments like headaches, sore joints, and cramps. While these fabrications increased demand, flannel was beyond many budgets.

In 1877, manufacturers figured out that if they brushed cotton, it would feel like flannel while being much cheaper to produce. Christening it "flannelette," they made even more money by selling this fake health trend to folks who could not afford the real thing.

But there was one big difference between the two textiles: flannel is a tightly woven wool and virtually fireproof, while flannelette is a soft, fluffy cotton and highly flammable.

Pyrotechnic Pajamas

At first, this new innovation seemed like an affordable way for less wealthy customers to keep their children healthy and warm in cozy sleepwear. Unfortunately, working-class homes relied on open flames for both heating and cooking. In typical cramped quarters, kids were always a few feet from fire. Not exactly the ideal place to be wearing a matchstick.

Not only could flannelette be set ablaze especially easily, but the fire, once started, spread astoundingly fast. A child could be engulfed in flames in seconds. Over a five-year period, 1,816 children burned to death while wearing flannelette in England alone. Older boys' styles were fitted, which significantly decreased their chances of catching fire. Girls were less lucky. Their loose, layered dresses provided a perfect fuse, and three-quarters of victims were girls.

LARGE.

d.I.X. SMALL.

C.C.S.Y. MEDIUM

C.C.S.Y. SMALL

BEFORE TEST

30 SECOND

60 SECOND
– 5 TIMES

BEFORE TEST

Before Test.

At 30 seconds.

At 60 seconds.

FLANNELETTE (ORDINARY)

Studies showed that untreated flannelette nightgowns burned to ashes after only sixty seconds.

Un-Flammable Flannelette

In 1900, a cotton manufacturer gave chemist William Henry Perkin Jr. a challenge. Could he invent something to make flannelette safe? Perkin was given four requirements:

1) Unchanged color and texture

2) Free of toxins like arsenic or lead

3) Able to withstand fifty wash cycles

4) Affordable for working-class consumers

It was difficult! Perkin did over ten thousand burn tests before he finally succeeded. He called his new fabric Non-Flam, short for "not flammable." The patent was donated to the British public so that every company could use it to make a safe product.

If you cannot get NONFLAM, the only flame proof Flannelette (Dr. Perkin's NONFLAM) do not accept a substitute, but write Patentees, WHIPP BROS., & TOD, LTD., 10, Aytoun St., Manchester.

Why is she not afraid of being burnt? Because she wears NONFLAM, the fire-resisting cosy, aseptic material, so strong'y recommended by Coroners.

BEFORE TEST

Poisonous Green

In 1775, chemist Carl Wilhelm Scheele invented an exceptionally vibrant green pigment that could be applied to clothing, wallpaper, toys, and even candy. This particular pigment has gone by a few names over the years—emerald green, Paris green, Scheele's green, and as a nod to one of its original ingredients, arsenic green.

Another name it goes by is poison green. Turns out arsenic is a highly toxic substance.

The Poisoned Wreath-Painter

Matilda Scheurer was a young woman of nineteen with a job at a London factory. All day long, she constructed wreaths of artificial flowers for fashionable ladies to wear in their hair. Matilda dusted green powdered pigment onto fake leaves with her bare hands. And on November 20, 1861, that green would kill her.

The press reported Matilda's demise in all its gruesome detail: Her fingernails and the whites of her eyes had turned green. She'd told her doctor that everything she looked at appeared green, before she vomited green water and stopped breathing.

The story alarmed the members of an organization called the Ladies' Sanitary Association. They decided to hire a world-famous chemist to figure out exactly what had happened.

An 1859 medical journal shows what happened to workers' hands after making imitation foliage dusted with arsenic.

The chemist published his findings in the London *Times*, and the news was not good: a single headdress contained enough arsenic to poison twenty people. He also found that a green gown could easily contain nine hundred grains of arsenic and shed sixty grains over the course of an evening of dancing. It would take only four or five grains to kill the average adult.

THE ARSENIC WALTZ.

THE NEW DANCE OF DEATH. (DEDICATED TO THE GREEN WREATH AND DRESS-MONGERS.)

Magazines published drawings of dead dancers to warn people about the dangers of dressing in green.

Throwing Shade on a Shade

Once its lethal potential went public, there was mass fear of all things green. Even after a nontoxic green dye was invented, no one wanted to wear it. Finally, in 1863, French empress Eugénie wore a brilliant green gown to the opera. Just as today's media goes wild when a movie star wears an attention-grabbing dress to the Oscars, the nineteenth-century press went crazy for it. After all the media coverage, people came around to the new, safe hue, named nouveau vert.

WHEN GREEN GOES MEAN

The connection between green dye and deadly arsenic is so deep it continues to pop up in pop culture today. Here are three characters that pair the color green with the idea of poison.

GREEN GOBLIN
When Norman Osborn was exposed to an unstable super-serum, he turned a shade of jade and became Spider-Man's unhinged adversary.

MOJO JOJO
The Powerpuff Girls' archenemy was just a regular monkey until Chemical X turned him into a green-faced evil genius.

MISTER YUK
Mr. Yuk stickers (BELOW) were developed in the 1970s to help kids recognize poisonous content.

POISON HELP!
©CHospPgh®
1-800-222-1222

Risky Radium

Marie Curie is considered such a hero that she was put on a French stamp. You can even visit her laboratory in Paris. Don't worry—it's decontaminated.

Nobody outside the scientific community paid much attention to the Nobel Prize in Physics before 1903, when, for the first time, the award went to a woman. Marie Curie's prize-winning discovery was a total media sensation. She had identified a mysterious new element that glowed and produced heat as if from nowhere. She called it radium.

Companies put the radium name on any product they thought would sell: razors, chocolate, perfume, children's books, and more. There was even a hit song called "The Radium Dance."

When researchers discovered that radium could help destroy cancer tumors, the health industry joined the promotional frenzy. The element was considered a cure-all medical miracle.

In 1928, that would change. Radium, as it turned out, was quite deadly.

Would You Wear Radioactive Underwear?

Radium was so outrageously expensive (it cost six thousand times more than gold), companies falsely claimed their goods contained the element. In an effort to "protect" consumers, the government fined anyone who exaggerated amounts of radium in anything they sold. For a price, Marie Curie's own laboratory would confirm radium content, literally stamping products with her approval.

Here are some wearable radium-containing products you could buy at the start of the twentieth century.

ORADIUM

The makers of this brand of wool suggested using their product to knit baby clothes and underwear, claiming the radioactivity had "undeniable hygienic value."

RADIOR

This British company's best-selling product was a pad sprinkled with radium, which customers strapped to their chins in the hopes that it would eradicate wrinkles.

THO-RADIA

This company marketed its lipstick as a "scientific beauty product," and promised its toothpaste, powder, and soap would give customers a "brighter smile and a glowing complexion."

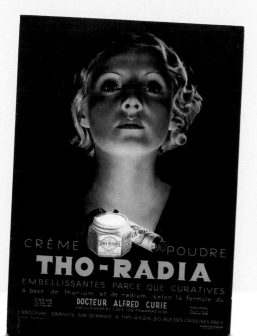

RADIATING STILL?

Radium is now banned from consumer products, but you never know where radioactive materials will turn up. In 2012, a black leather belt decorated with 801 metal studs, sold by online clothing retailer ASOS, set off bomb control sensors at the US border. The metal contained enough radioactive cobalt to cause health problems if worn for more than five hundred hours. ASOS turned over its inventory, which is currently confined to a protective storage facility.

29

The Radium Girls

In 1914, the fastest way to tell time was to check your wristwatch. This option was limited to daylight hours, of course—it was pretty hard to see a watch in the dark. That is, until the invention of Undark brand radium paint. Lit up with a greenish-white glow, a radium-painted watch could tell you the time ... anytime!

Hundreds of American teenage girls, many as young as fourteen, worked in factories painting these watches. The clockfaces were very small, and a sharp brush was essential for producing the required fine lines. The young women were taught to shape the radium-covered bristles on their tongues and lips.

They were assured the paint was safe, and they each completed an average of 250 watches a day. Sometimes they would even play with the radium, giving their fingernails, teeth, and eyelashes a brilliant glow with a few coats.

Women and even teenage girls spent long days painting alarm clocks and watch faces with glowing, lethal radium.

The Sins of the US Radium Corporation

The first to fall seriously ill was Mollie Maggia. No one was able to figure out why. Her teeth were pulled in hopes of stopping the spread of infection, but once her jawbone crumbled in a doctor's hands, they knew it was hopeless. Maggia died on September 12, 1922, five years after she'd started working at a watch factory. She was twenty-four.

More women's teeth began to fall out. The US Radium Corporation, where Maggia had worked, refused to accept responsibility for anyone's illness. They would continue the denial for years, even though their own secret investigations had turned up conclusive evidence: radium was most certainly harming their staff.

It was only when a male employee died that an autopsy was done. The doctors learned that the body mistakes radium for calcium, and when ingested, the toxic substance ends up in the bones. These young women were being destroyed from the inside by what would come to be called radium poisoning.

Glowing in Their Graves

Maggia's coworker Grace Fryer was eighteen when she started painting watches at the factory. Years later, in a new job, she was showing signs of radium poisoning. She knew what was ahead of her, having seen many of her coworkers succumb to the illness. She wanted to hold the company accountable for its negligence, but even more, she wanted to warn the women still putting radium in their mouths every day. With four other workers, she decided to sue. The 1928 court case attracted massive national press attention, spreading word across the country of the women's story and the risks of radium.

They won their case. It was the first time that courts had ever held a company responsible for the health of its employees. Soon after, the national government established life-saving laws. These five young women, dubbed the "Radium Girls" by the press, changed history. When they died, all before the age of thirty, they had to be buried in lead caskets. Their bodies remain radioactive to this day.

Factory Catastrophes

On Tuesday, Beyoncé is photographed in a T-shirt. The next weekend, a copy of that T-shirt is on sale at the mall for twelve dollars. This is what we call fast fashion.

Fast fashion is a fairly new expression, but it's hardly a twenty-first century idea. Consumers have long wanted to pay less for more. This pressure has more often than not meant that in many places around the world and at many times throughout history, much of our clothing is made by employees who have been overworked, underpaid, and subject to unsafe conditions. And this dire situation continues today.

Separated by thousands of miles and more than a hundred years, the Triangle Shirtwaist Factory fire in the US and the Rana Plaza collapse in Bangladesh were strikingly similar. Their workers were young, poor immigrants and migrants, and they were mostly women. They worked twelve hours a day, seven days a week. In the wake of these tragedies, workers fought to make sure that your cheap T-shirt doesn't cost their lives.

Triangle Shirtwaist Factory Fire

WHERE: New York City, US

WHEN: March 25, 1911

WAGE: US$6 a month (equal to $150 today)

WHAT HAPPENED: When the fire started on the eighth floor, the factory's nearly five hundred workers frantically tried to escape. There were two exits to the street, but the factory owners had locked one to prevent theft. The other door opened inward, and within three minutes, the crush of bodies made it impossible to budge. Some tried to use the fire escape, but it was so poorly constructed that it collapsed and killed twenty people. Many chose to jump out windows rather than burn.

BODY COUNT: 146 dead, 71 injured

AFTERMATH: Factory owners Isaac Harris and Max Blanck were charged with manslaughter, but they were found not guilty. In a later civil suit, they were ordered to pay the families $75 per deceased victim. The owners then collected an insurance payout of $65,000, or $445 per victim. In 1913, Blanck was once again arrested for locking the door in his factory during working hours. He was fined $20.

FIGHTING FOR CHANGE: The city's grief quickly turned to outrage after a mass funeral and a clothing workers' meeting. The International Ladies' Garment Workers' Union persuaded New York State to enact laws that would inspire changes to the whole country's regulations.

Rana Plaza Collapse

WHERE: Savar, Bangladesh

WHEN: April 24, 2013

WAGE: US$38 a month

WHAT HAPPENED: The night before the collapse, large cracks were found in the building's support columns. The main floor bank was evacuated, but the garment workers on the upper floors were ordered to return to work the next day or lose their month's pay. Vibrations from a generator triggered the eight-story collapse first thing in the morning. It only took ninety seconds for hundreds of people to be trapped in the rubble. Rescue efforts continued until the last survivor was pulled out, seventeen days after the collapse.

BODY COUNT: 1,134 dead, more than 2,500 injured

AFTERMATH: Four days after the collapse, owner Sohel Rana was arrested attempting to cross the Indian border. As of 2018, he awaits a murder trial, although in 2017 he was convicted of corruption and sentenced to three years in prison.

FIGHTING FOR CHANGE: Thousands of garment workers immediately took to the streets demanding better working conditions. As a result, seven safety inspectors were suspended and eighteen factories closed.

Part Three

Unlucky Legs

Restrictive Skirts

In 1908, Edith Berg was the first woman to fly in a plane. But when she climbed aboard the Wright brothers' *Flyer*, she discovered a problem: the open-air cockpit provided no protection from the intense wind, and her large skirt was sure to fly up in her face. Undeterred, she grabbed a length of twine and tied it around her knees.

The unusual shape created by this last-minute fix inspired a fashion trend. Women started wearing a new, narrow skirt style that cinched at the knees or even the ankles. The design might have been useful for flying, but it made simple walking a real pain. Unlike pilots soaring through the skies, the wearers of these new "aeroplane dresses" could take only one teeny, tiny step at a time.

Because it effectively shackled its wearers, the new dress was named after a device used to keep animals from running away: the hobble.

Lady and the Tramp(led)

Alas, the hobble skirt caused countless injuries and, occasionally, was even lethal. In 1910 at a Paris racecourse, a horse (which ironically wasn't properly hobbled) got loose and bolted into a crowd of spectators. One woman wearing a hobble skirt couldn't get out of the way in time and was tragically trampled to death. A year later, the hobble skirt of an eighteen-year-old girl caused her to trip while stepping over a locked gate on a canal lock, and she fell into the icy water below. It turned out the hobble wasn't very good for swimming in either. She drowned.

DID YOU KNOW?

The distinctive shape of the iconic Coca-Cola bottle was inspired by the hobble skirt.

THE FASHION OF THE MOMENT AS A SUBSTITUTE FOR THE SACK: "LA COURSE D'ENTRAVÉES."

DRAWN BY RENÉ LELONG.

THE ILLUSTRATED LONDON NEWS, AUG. 13, 1910.—243

A "SACK-RACE" FOR WEARERS OF "HOBBLE" SKIRTS: LADIES IN A SPEED CONTEST.

It has been said with a good deal of truth that wearers of the "tube" frock in its most exaggerated form are so hobbled by the tightness of their skirts that they find it difficult to walk, save with the shortest and most mincing of steps, practically impossible to run, and exceedingly difficult to go up and down stairs, or to enter a motor-car or other vehicle. It has been remarked several times, indeed, that the movements of the ladies in question suggest a sack-race rather than anything else. This notion so appealed to the committee organising a fête in a French suburb the tight skirts in question. This, of course, was a speed contest, the skirts of the competitors must not be more than 1 met be noted, ran as best they could; others hopped, kan

> Hobble skirts were often mocked for their impracticality. A joke "race" was held, and postcards made fun of a woman unable to get over a fence in the garment.

THE HOBBLE SKIRT.
"WHAT'S THAT? OH, IT'S THE SPEED-LIMIT SKIRT AGAIN."

THE HOBBLE SKIRT.
"MY WORD! HERE'S A GO!"

THE HOBBLE SKIRT.
"ALTOGETHER BOYS!"

Deadly Denim Distress

Every day, almost half of the world's population wears blue jeans. The familiar design was invented in 1873 by Jacob Davis, and the pants were first manufactured in America by Levi Strauss & Co. They were instantly popular with cowboys, miners, and dockworkers, who all needed pants that were tough. It took a lot of work to rip or rough up a pair of jeans.

A hundred years later, jeans would be valued less for their ability not to fade, and more for how good they looked once they were faded. Denim designers accelerated deterioration by washing the pants with acid or stones, and in the early 2000s, they discovered sandblasting. Originally invented to clean the outside of stone buildings, the technique could also rapidly age brand-new denim by literally blasting it with sand from a hose.

Sandblasting jeans is fast, cheap, and effective. It is also frequently fatal.

Unprotected Sandblasting

Faysal Demir was only twenty when he left his small Turkish village of Taşlıçay in 2002. Jean manufacturing was booming in Istanbul; the industry was selling $2 billion worth of the product every year. This incredible demand meant jobs for the country's desperate workers, who flocked from all over to the big city. Demir was soon followed by his eight brothers.

Given only a simple and wholly ineffectual facemask as protection, Demir was told to sandblast denim daily in an enclosed and poorly ventilated room. By 2004, he was beginning to feel unwell. Tired and short of breath, he complained of a cough that would not go away.

He didn't know that two fellow jean workers, teenagers also from Taşlıçay, had recently sought medical treatment for their own breathing troubles. The doctors were able to provide the first of what would become a common diagnosis: silicosis.

Diagnosis: Silicosis
Prognosis? Death

The sand you find on a beach contains tiny silica grains invisible to the eye. When inhaled, these particles damage the lungs. The more sand is inhaled, and the longer it's inhaled for, the harder it is to breathe. Eventually, breathing becomes impossible.

After sandblasting jeans eleven hours a day for three years, the teenagers had advanced silicosis. Doctors would confirm thousands more sufferers, with three hundred of those—including all nine of the Demir brothers—in tiny Taşlıçay. The Turkish government finally banned denim sandblasting in 2009, but hundreds still die every year, including Faysal Demir in December of 2017.

Disappointingly, the Turkish ban did not stop sandblasting altogether. The unsafe practice was instead taken up in poorer, less regulated countries.

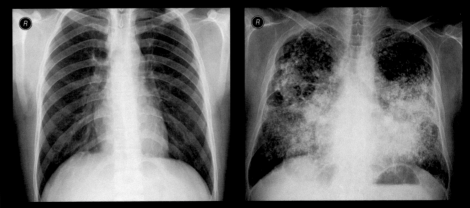

Dr. Metin Akgün helped get the Turkish sandblasting ban put in place. He showed the difference between healthy lungs (left) and the sick lungs of his patients (right). The white "clouds" on the right are the permanent scars from breathing in sand.

39

Fatal Footwear Fiascos

Impractical shoes have caused countless twisted ankles, an untold number of broken bones, and in a few instances … death.

One Foot in the Grave

The year 1999 was unlucky for women wearing platform shoes in Japan. That year, a twenty-five-year-old nursery school employee was found dead. Authorities put together that she had tripped and badly fractured her skull while wearing a pair of ten-inch-tall cork sandals. She managed to make it to her car, but then fell unconscious and eventually died from her injuries before she was able to get medical attention.

A few months later, a different twenty-five-year-old woman was driving home from a shopping trip. Her eight-inch-high boots made it difficult to use the brake, and she crashed the car into a concrete pole. She survived, but her friend in the passenger seat did not. As a result, Japanese police banned wearing platform shoes while driving, declaring the practice as dangerous as talking on a cell phone.

Harrowing Heels

Carlisle Champalimaud was planning on staying at a friend's New York City apartment one night in 2012, but she never made it inside. Her body was found the next morning at the bottom of a flight of stairs she had attempted to navigate in very high heels while carrying a heavy overnight bag.

UNFORTUNATE FAIRY TALE FOOTWEAR

The land of make-believe is full of miserable stories about magical shoes.

SNOW WHITE

Very Shortened Plot: Wicked queen orders the murder of her more-beautiful stepdaughter, who narrowly escapes and hides out with some little people in the woods.

Gruesome Shoe Scene: In the Grimm brothers' version, the queen is punished for her wickedness by being forced to dance to death in red-hot iron shoes.

CINDERELLA

Very Shortened Plot: Girl has some pretty mean stepsisters, goes to a fancy dance party, meets a prince, and loses a slipper.

Gruesome Shoe Scene: In darker versions of the story, the prince declares he will marry whoever fits in the lost slipper, and the stepsisters unsuccessfully try to trick him by cutting off their toes and heels.

THE RED SHOES

Very Shortened Plot: A little orphan named Karen is given some red shoes. She's not allowed to wear them to church, but she does anyway.

Gruesome Shoe Scene: As a punishment for her disobedience, Karen can't stop dancing. She convinces a man with an axe to chop off her feet so she can finally rest.

Blazing Ballerinas

In 1809, a miraculous machine was invented that could make yards of tulle netting in mere minutes. The fabric's simple honeycomb pattern was practically weightless and made dancing look like floating. Soon, ballerinas everywhere wouldn't be caught dead without a tutu made of tulle … until they were caught dead in it.

A young lady rescues her friend by throwing a thick woolen "fire" blanket over her ball gown to smother the flames.

Fire Dance with Me

Before electricity was invented, theaters were illuminated with gas lamps. Wooden buildings and open-flamed lights proved to be a catastrophic combination. From 1797 to 1897, there were more than five hundred theater fires worldwide, with casualties exceeding ten thousand.

During ballet performances, stage floors were lined with footlights so the flickering flames could draw attention to dancers' legs. Tulle's loose and airy construction was great for dancing, but it was also great kindling. When a dancer got too close to the fire, her poufy dress became a puff of smoke.

Burn Out

In 1859, French authorities tried to stop ballerinas from burning by passing a law requiring all costumes to be coated with alum, borax, and boric acid. The chemical compound prevented the tulle from catching fire, but it also gave it a yellowed, stiff, and dingy look.

Beloved ballerina Emma Livry refused to wear the treated tutus. On November 15, 1862, as she waited to dance a dress rehearsal, her skirt got too

The dramatic and tragic backstage blaze that killed the Gale sisters was recreated in an American newspaper illustration.

close to a footlight. Instantly, she was engulfed in flames three times her height. She ran onstage, but by the time they put her out with a blanket, she had already suffered burns over 40 percent of her body. She died months later in terrible pain.

Safety regulations were finally put into place. Every theater was equipped with large water tanks and wet blankets backstage to avoid a repeat performance of the dancer's gruesome fate.

THE SAD TALE OF THE SISTERS GALE

One September evening in 1861, the audience in a crowded Philadelphia theater impatiently waited for a ballet performance to begin. Little did they know tragedy was about to strike.

That night, fourteen-year-old ballerina Cecilia Gale and her three sisters were rushing around backstage, getting ready to dance. In Cecilia's haste, she brushed against a flame. Seconds later she was on fire. Her fellow dancers all rushed to help her, but as soon as they got close, their costumes were also set ablaze. In the end, six ballerinas perished, including all four sisters.

43

Don't Blame the Victim

In this book, we use the words "unfortunate" and "unlucky" quite a few times. Perhaps this isn't surprising, since we're dealing with the many ways that the quest for beauty can kill.

These words mean the same thing: a twist of fate with an unfavorable outcome. And it's true that many of the people in this book had bad luck. Terrible luck. But is bad luck the only reason for all of these deaths? Unfortunately, no.

Sometimes the cause of death was vanity. People valued their appearance more than their health and safety. Men and women in Elizabethan England kept slathering their faces with lead-tainted paint long after they knew it caused skin to rot. Teetering on extremely high heels or squeezing into leg-binding hobble skirts were obvious risks, most likely taken deliberately.

Yet sometimes the risks were less clear. Families in the late Victorian era who could not afford real wool flannel wanted to keep their children warm. But they couldn't have known that cotton flannelette—sold to them as a healthy substitute—would turn out to be a fire hazard. After its discovery, radium was widely advertised as beneficial. Why would anyone have suspected it could melt you from the inside out?

But the biggest risks in this book were always taken by those most desperate for a better life. Sadly, that motivation compelled people to work in unsafe conditions making hats or hair decorations or cheap T-shirts. Or to cram into a boat setting out for a new land, even if getting there meant risking deadly illnesses transmitted by the bugs living in their clothes.

In the present day, hatters aren't mad and faces don't fall off from wearing thick foundation. The chances of being poisoned by an arsenic-laced ball gown are extremely small. So what changed?

Sometimes these risks were eliminated by chance. Electric lights were not invented to save dancers, but we don't hear about combusting ballerinas anymore. And when washing machines started saving labor, they also started saving lives. Typhus was once rampant, but now it is rare.

Other times, once exposed, risks were considered unacceptable. Companies and governments were forced to make changes. Factory tragedies such as the Triangle Shirtwaist fire inspired new and better regulations that have since made many workplaces safer. (Although as the Rana Plaza collapse shows, the most desperate among us, such as undocumented workers and people in developing nations, remain vulnerable.) When new cosmetics, medicines, and chemicals are invented, medical standards and government regulations demand that they be tested extensively before they can be brought to the market.

We can reduce the body count of killer styles. Declare the risks unacceptable. Mind the most vulnerable.

And absolutely, for sure, beyond a doubt . . . *don't* wear a scarf when riding a go-kart.

Sources

BIBLIOGRAPHY

AGINS, TERI. *The End of Fashion: How Marketing Changed the Clothing Business Forever*. New York: Quill, 2000.

AKGÜN, METIN, et. al. "An Epidemic of Silicosis Among Former Denim Sandblasters." In *European Respirology Journal* 32 (2008): 1295–1303.

ALDERSEY-WILLIAMS, HUGH. *Periodic Tales: The Curious Lives of the Elements*. London: Viking, 2011.

ALI MANIK, JULFIKAR, AND JIM YARDLEY. "Garment Workers Stage Angry Protest after Bangladesh Fire." *New York Times*, November 26, 2012. Online.

BLANC, PAUL D. *How Everyday Products Make People Sick: Toxins at Home and in the Workplace*. Oakland: University of California Press, 2009.

BRONSTEIN, JAMIE L. *Caught in the Machinery: Workplace Accidents and Injured Workers in Nineteenth-Century Britain*. Stanford: Stanford University Press, 2008.

CHIPMAN, IAN. "How to Improve Working Conditions in the Developing World." *Insights by Stanford Business* (Stanford Graduate School of Business), August 10, 2016. Online.

CLINE, ELIZABETH L. *Over-Dressed: The Shockingly High Cost of Cheap Fashion*. New York: Portfolio/Penguin, 2012.

CORSON, RICHARD. *Fashions in Makeup: From Ancient to Modern Times*. New York: Universe Books, 1972.

FAIR TRADE CENTER. *Fashion Victims: A Report on Sandblasted Denim* (Stockholm: Fair Trade Center), November 2010. Online.

GREENPEACE. *Toxic Threads: The Big Fashion Stitch-Up* (Amsterdam: Greenpeace International), 2012. Online.

LEE, MICHELLE. *Fashion Victim: Our Love-Hate Relationship with Dressing, Shopping, and the Cost of Style*. New York: Broadway, 2003.

MATTHEWS DAVID, ALISON. *Fashion Victims: The Dangers of Dress Past and Present*. London: Bloomsbury, 2015.

McGOWAN, MARK G. *Death or Canada: The Irish Famine Migration to Toronto, 1847*. Toronto: Novalis, 2009.

McNEIL, DONALD G., JR. "Turkey: Sandblasting Jeans for 'Distressed' Look Proved Harmful for Textile Workers." *New York Times*, October 31, 2011. Online.

MOORE, KATE. *The Radium Girls: The Dark Story of America's Shining Women*. Naperville, Illinois: Sourcebooks, 2017.

OLSON, KELLY. *Dress and the Roman Woman: Self-Presentation and Society*. New York: Routledge, 2008.

ORCI, TAYLOR. "The Original 'Blonde Bombshell' Used Actual Bleach on Her Head." *Atlantic*, February 22, 2013. Online.

PASTOUREAU, MICHEL. *Green: The History of a Color*. Princeton: Princeton University Press, 2014.

SHAH, MANTHAN P., et. al. "Lead Content of Sindoor, a Hindu Religious Powder and Cosmetic: New Jersey and India, 2014–2015." *American Journal of Public Health* 107, no. 10 (2017): 1630–1632.

SIEGLE, LUCY. *To Die For: Is Fashion Wearing Out the World?* London: Fourth Estate, 2011.

STEELE, VALERIE. *The Corset: A Cultural History*. New Haven, CT: Yale University Press, 2001.

STILLMAN, SARAH. "Death Traps: The Bangladesh Garment-Factory Disaster." *New Yorker*, May 1, 2013. Online.

THOMAS, DANA. *Deluxe: How Luxury Lost Its Luster*. New York: Penguin, 2008.

VINCENT, SUSAN J. *The Anatomy of Fashion: Dressing the Body from the Renaissance to Today*. Oxford: Berg, 2009.

VON DREHLE, DAVID. *Triangle: The Fire That Changed America*. New York: Grove Press, 2003.

WHORTON, JAMES C. *The Arsenic Century: How Victorian Britain Was Poisoned at Home, Work, and Play*. Oxford: Oxford University Press, 2010.

ZINSSER, HANS. *Rats, Lice and History: Being a Study in Biography, Which, after Twelve Preliminary Chapters Indispensable for the Preparation of the Lay Reader, Deals with the Life History of Typhus Fever*. Boston: Little, Brown and Company, 1935.